To Dr Isaac H. Manning
with deep respect and admir...
May 3 - 71

Wellsprings of Wisdom

When the pilgrim of truth
comes on his journey
to the region of the parable,
he finds its interpretation.
It is not a fruit or a jewel
to be stored, but a well
springing by the wayside.

GEORGE MACDONALD

The rarest and mightiest
possession of the human spirit
can be discovered
only by means of story
and by no other process of thinking—
to know all this
and to have it as your own
is to have much.

GORDON KEITH CHALMERS

*Fascinating stories and parables
that guide and inspire*

Wellsprings
of Wisdom

WRITTEN AND COMPILED BY

Ralph L. Woods

THE C. R. GIBSON COMPANY
NORWALK, CONNECTICUT

Copyright © MCMLXIX by The C. R. Gibson Company
All rights reserved
Printed in the United States of America
Library of Congress Catalog Card Number: 68–23433
Standard Book Number: 8378–1779–X

*A complete list of acknowledgments
will be found at the end of this book*

Contents

Man Sees Himself **1**

Just stand aside and watch yourself go by,
Think of yourself as "he" instead of "I"

Humility

A tired farmer, oppressed by the noonday heat, sat under a walnut tree for some rest, and as he sat there he looked at his pumpkin vines and said to himself, "God is really very foolish and inexperienced. He puts big heavy pumpkins on a frail vine that has so little strength it has to lie on the ground. And then he puts small walnuts on a big tree with branches that can hold a man. Any man could do better than that!"

Just then a breeze dislodged a walnut from the tree under which the farmer sat, and the walnut fell on the critic's head. The old man rubbed his head ruefully and said, "It's a good thing there wasn't a pumpkin up there instead of a walnut."

Shortsighted

An ambitious farmer, unhappy about the yield of his crops, heard of a highly recommended new seed corn. He bought some and produced a crop that was so abundant his astonished neighbors came and asked him to sell them some of the new seed. But the farmer, afraid that he would lose a profitable competitive advantage, refused to sell the seed to his neighbors.

The second year the new seed did not produce quite so good a crop for the farmer. And when the third-year crop was still worse, it suddenly dawned upon the farmer that his prize corn was being pollinated by the inferior grade of corn from his neighbors' fields.

Fame

Enrico Caruso, the world famous operatic tenor, was driving through the Wisconsin countryside while on a concert tour when he realized he was well lost. He stopped at a farmhouse for directions and a drink of water, and became friendly with the farmer and the great singer was invited to stay for the mid-day meal then being put on the table. As he was preparing to leave after a fine meal Caruso thought it would please the kindly old farmer and his wife to know that they had entertained so celebrated a personality, so he told them his name.

The farmer was wide-eyed. "This is a great thing," he said. "Who would have thought that I would have as a guest that great explorer—Robinson Crusoe!"

Positive Thinking

Some years ago two competing salesmen for shoe manufacturers arrived simultaneously in Africa to develop markets for their companies. Both men headed for the unexploited interior. After a few weeks one of the salesmen cabled his company that he was returning home on the next boat because of the lack of sales opportunities since the natives did not wear shoes.

The other salesman at about the same time sent off this terse cable to his company: "Send quick millions of pairs of shoes all sizes, colors, styles because the natives here have no shoes."

An Eloquent Reply

A watch-maker in England determined that he would do work that was more exquisitely delicate even than that of his Swiss competitors. Finally, he perfected a strand of wire he was confident could not be duplicated by any other watch-maker—it was, he assured himself, the thinnest man could make. He placed this wire in a velvet-lined box and sent it to a Swiss watch manufacturer with a note explaining it was a sample of the kind of work he was doing in England.

Several weeks later the man in England received a small package from Switzerland. It, too, was a velvet-lined jewel box. It contained the tiny wire sent from England. And alongside it was a jeweler's lens. Puzzled, the man put the lens to his eye and looked at the hair-like strand of wire. He then discovered that the Swiss watch-maker had drilled a neat hole through the center of the delicate wire.

Gratitude

An ambitious young man called on his pastor and promised to tithe, and so together they knelt in prayer to make the promise and to ask God's blessing on the young fellow's career. He was only making forty dollars a week at that time, and therefore tithed four dollars. But before many years his income leaped into higher brackets and he was tithing as much as $500 a week. He decided he had better call on the minister and see if he could not somehow be released from his tithing promise—it was getting much too costly. He told the pastor, "It was no problem when I was only tithing four dollars every week—but now it is up to five hundred dollars—and I simply can't afford that."

The old pastor said, "I do not see how you can be released from your promise, but we could kneel down now and ask God to cut your income back to about forty dollars and a tithe of four dollars a week."

Pride

A king was told that a man of humility is endowed with long life. He attired himself in old garments, took up his residence in a small hut, and forbade anyone to show reverence before him. But when he honestly examined himself, the King found himself to be prouder of his seeming humility than ever before. A philosopher thereupon remarked to him: "Dress like a king; live like a king; allow the people to show due respect to you; but be humble in your inmost heart."

THE BAALSHEM

The Ideal House

When a man and his wife bought their house in the suburbs it had everything they desired—space, light, view, design, stability of neighborhood, location.

But after several years the couple began to find fault with their house—mostly trivial objections that they allowed to assume importance. So they decided to put their house up for sale, and then search for their dream house. They turned the sale over to a real estate man, while they looked for their ideal.

One day they read an advertisement describing exactly the kind of a house they wanted. They phoned the real estate man and discovered the advertisement was one for their own house—the one they were endeavoring to sell.

Humility

A young student of the piano went to Europe on a summer vacation and visited the home of Beethoven and asked the guard for permission to play on the great master's piano. When she had played a few bars she turned to the guard and said, "No doubt all the great artists play this piano when they visit here?"

"No," replied the guard. "All the great contemporary pianists have visited here, but none of them so much as touched the piano. They did not feel worthy to do so. I have found that all the truly great are humble. Perhaps that is part of their greatness."

Gift and Reward

I had gone a-begging from door to door in the village path, when thy golden chariot appeared in the distance like a gorgeous dream and I wondered who was this King of all kings!

My hopes rose high and methought my evil days were at an end, and stood waiting for alms to be given unasked and for wealth scattered on all sides in the dust.

The chariot stopped where I stood. Thy glance fell on me and thou camest down with a smile. I felt that the luck of my life had come at last. Then of a sudden thou didst hold out thy right hand and say, "What hast thou to give me?"

Ah, what a kingly jest it was to open thy palm to a beggar to beg! I was confused and stood undecided, and then from my wallet I slowly took out the least little grain of corn and gave it to thee.

But how great my surprise when at the day's end I emptied my bag on the floor to find a least little grain of gold among the poor heap! I bitterly wept and wished that I had the heart to give thee my all.

RABINDRANATH TAGORE

Sometimes Worry Helps

A stout man went in search of his vagrant puppy, and finally traced its whining plea for help to a no-longer used conduit in the woods. The frightened animal either could not or would not leave his hiding place.

The man decided to go after his little dog, and forced his bulky body into the conduit but then found himself so tightly wedged in that he could no longer move forward or backward. He realized he could die in this situation, and the thought of it terrified him.

In this desperate predicament the man began to think of his family: how improvident he had been and how little money he had put aside for his wife and children. The more he thought about this the more the family's welfare worried him, and the more he worried the more he perspired. Finally, after hours of extreme worry and great perspiration, he had lost so much weight that he was able to crawl out of the conduit—a man now full of good resolutions.

Gratitude

I had never complained of the vicissitudes of fortune, nor murmured at the ordinances of heaven, excepting on one occasion, when my feet were bare and I had not the wherewithal to shoe them. In this desponding state I entered the metropolitan mosque at Cufah, and there beheld a man who had no feet. I offered up praise and thanksgiving for God's goodness to myself, and submitted with patience to my want of shoes.

SA'DI

Treasure at Hand

A certain man of Baghdad dreamed one night that in a certain house in a certain street in Cairo he should find a treasure. To Egypt accordingly he went, and met in the desert with one who was on his road from Cairo to Baghdad, having dreamt that in a certain house in a certain street he should find the treasure; and lo, each of these men had been directed to the other's house to find a treasure that only needed looking for in his own.

From the Persian by EDWARD FITZGERALD

Practicality

Thomas A. Edison once hired a young engineer, just graduated from a fine college. He told the young expert to determine the cubic content of a light bulb. After a day of careful measurement and mathematical calculations the young engineer went to the famous inventor and proudly told him the answer he had arrived at.

But Edison said, "No, that is not correct." He picked up a light bulb, gently knocked a tiny hole in the end of it, and filled the bulb with water. Then he poured the water into a measuring cup and quickly proved that his expert's answer was about twelve per cent off.

Know Thyself

A prosperous young Wall Street broker met, fell in love with and was frequently seen escorting about town a rising actress of gentility and dignity. He wanted to marry her, but being a cautious man he decided that before proposing matrimony he should have a private investigating agency check her background and present activities. After all, he reminded himself, I have both a growing fortune and my reputation to protect against a marital misadventure.

The Wall Streeter requested that the agency was not to reveal to the investigator the identity of the client requesting a report on the actress.

In due time the investigator's report was sent to the

broker. It said the actress had an unblemished past, a spotless reputation, and her friends and associates were of the best repute. "The only shadow," added the report, "is that currently she is often seen around town in the company of a young broker of dubious business practices and principles."

Spiritual Blindness

A man who had spent all of his time making and hoarding money found himself in a most disturbed and unhappy state, and went to a minister for counsel.

The minister, who knew the man rather well, picked up the Bible, pointed to the word "God" and asked, "Can you see that?"

"Certainly," replied the man with annoyance.

"All right," said the minister as he picked up a coin and placed it over the word "God." "Can you see the word now?"

The man did not reply immediately, but presently he said "Yes, I understand now."

The Scandalmonger

For many years a man who had taken pleasure in spreading scandalous and often untrue stories about his friends and acquaintances, himself became the victim of a nasty story. Suddenly he realized the anguish and injury he must have caused others by the damaging tales he had long been putting into circulation. He went to the village sage and explained that he wanted to repair the damage he had done—he wanted to re-call the stories he had spread.

"First you must catch a goose," said the wise man. "Then strip it of its feathers, and scatter them to the four winds. Then you must recover every feather."

"But, sir," protested the tale-bearer, "I can't possibly do that. The feathers could never be recovered."

"Neither," replied the sage, "can you call back the stories you have spread, or undo the harm done."

The Man Who Fooled Himself

A big professional gambler, wintering and betting on the horses in Florida, decided to concentrate on a cer-tain horse in a certain race on a certain day. He knew the horse would be the betting favorite. But in order to discourage so many people from betting on this par-ticular horse, which could make the winning price smaller, the gambler mentioned to a tout that one of the longer-priced horses in the same race was an excel-lent bet. It was a good deal faster than the handicap-pers or the public realized. It had a good jockey, the horse was ready to win and the owner was out to win with him.

As the gambler expected, the tout passed this infor-mation around, giving his source as the big gambler who was in-the-know. Before very long quite a few people at the track had decided to bet on this "dark horse," and as the word spread the story was embroidered beyond all reason. Consequently the odds lengthened on the favorite on which the gambler planned to bet.

Eventually, however, the tout's story came back to the gambler in a far more attractive form than when he launched it. In fact, the gambler did not even recognize it as his own yarn. He was so impressed by what he heard that at the last minute he changed his mind and switched from the favorite to the widely touted horse. The favorite won, and the dark horse finished last.

Fame

He had come to the big city from a little rural community, had worked hard and intelligently and climbed high up the business ladder with unusual speed. He was, in fact, rather well-known among businessmen in the big town.

With the means and freedom now to indulge himself, he thought of the home-town and how nice it would be to return for a visit—a visit no doubt characterized by praise and adulation of the local boy who had made the big time.

When he stepped off the train there was no welcoming committee there to greet him. This was surprising, and a bit disconcerting. The few people on the station platform paid him no heed and went on their way. As he picked up his bag an old freight handler came up, looked at him curiously and said, "Howdy Jim, you leavin' town?"

Pleasure

A boy, greatly smitten by the colors of a butterfly, pursued it from flower to flower. First he tried to surprise it among the leaves of a rose; then he tried to cover it with his hat when it was feeding on a daisy. Again he hoped to capture it when he found it loitering among violets. But the fickle butterfly, continually changing from one blossom to another, still eluded the lad's attempts. Finally, noticing it buried in the cup of a tulip, the boy reached forward and snatched it with such violence that the butterfly was crushed to pieces. The dying insect spoke to the boy with all the calmness of a stoic: "Behold now the end of thy unprofitable solicitude! And learn that all pleasure is but a painted butterfly, which, although it may serve thee in the pursuit, if embraced with too much ardour, will perish in thy grasp."

Willing Servant

A diplomat called on President Lincoln and found him blacking his shoes. When he expressed astonishment that the President of the United States would black his own shoes, Lincoln looked up at him and said, "And whose shoes do you black?"

Man Encounters Life 2

Be such a man, and live such a life,
that if every man were such as you,
and every life a life like yours,
this earth would be God's Paradise.

You Can't Please Everyone

A man who decided to take his donkey to town to sell it, started off with his son and himself walking alongside the animal. They had not gone very far when they met a group of young girls returning from town. "Look at that old fool!" one of the girls cried out. "At least one of them could ride the donkey but there they are walking." So the father put his son on the donkey and continued the trip.

Presently they passed a group of women who stood chatting outside a house. "There, that proves what I've been saying," said one of the women in a loud voice. "Look at that young brat riding the donkey while his poor father is walking. We're spoiling our children!" When the father heard this he thought perhaps he had better avoid further criticism by taking the son's place on the donkey's back.

As they neared the town they met an aggressive young woman who stopped and denounced the father as being cruel. "How can you ride the animal while your poor little boy has to trudge along beside you in the dust and heat!" With a sigh the poor man told the son to mount the donkey, too, and thus burdened the poor beast struggled along toward town.

When they entered the town a bustling citizen dashed up to them and cried out: "You ought to be reported—two big healthy people sitting up there on that poor animal's back. Why you two should be carrying the donkey instead of it carrying you!" The alarmed father dismounted with his son and they tied the animal's legs and with a pole across their shoulders struggled along with the donkey, until they came to a bridge, where a number of people began laughing uproariously at them. This noise frightened the donkey and he fought to free himself. This increased the uproar of the crowd and in the midst of it all the animal slipped off the pole and over the bridge into the river below, and drowned.

AESOP

Crossing the River

Many years ago, when I was a young lawyer, and Illinois was little settled, except on her southern border, I, with other lawyers, used to ride the circuit; journeying with the judge from county-seat to county-seat in quest of business. Once, after a long spell of pouring rain, which had flooded the whole country, transforming small creeks into rivers, we were often stopped by these swollen streams, which were with difficulty crossed. Still ahead of us was the Fox River, larger than all the rest; and we could not help saying to each other, "If these streams give us so much trouble, how shall we get across Fox River?" Darkness fell before we had reached that stream; and we all stopped at a log tavern, had our horses put out, and resolved to pass the night. Here we were right glad to fall in with the Methodist Presiding Elder of the Circuit [Peter

Cartwright], who rode it in all weather, knew all its ways, and could tell us all about Fox River. So we all gathered around him, and asked him if he knew about the crossing of Fox River. "Oh, yes," he replied, "I know all about Fox River. I have crossed it often and understand it well; but I have one fixed rule with regard to Fox River: I never cross it till I reach it."

ABRAHAM LINCOLN

Troubles

Years ago the inhabitants of a small town got into the habit of constantly complaining about their problems, troubles, difficulties—real and imaginary. It was a soured, unhappy community. When the condition kept getting worse, an angel appeared, gave to each person in the community a bag and instructed that each one should put all his troubles in his bag and then hang the bag on the picket fence surrounding the village church. At a given signal the villagers were then to run at their top speed and pick out whichever bag of troubles they wanted.

The scramble, confusion and fighting that resulted was extraordinary—especially since each person wanted only to get back his own bag of troubles.

Initiative

Years ago a friend asked the famous inventor Charles F. Kettering if it was true that he went from Detroit to Dayton in four and a half hours without breaking the speed laws. Kettering said it was true, and he suggested the friend follow him the next time he made the trip. The friend did so and they reached Dayton in four and a half hours, never exceeding the speed limit. The friend was annoyed. "You didn't take Route 25," he said.

Kettering told his irate friend that when a man wants to get somewhere fast he should never take Route 25, but always the road of his own choosing.

Free Lunch

The friends of a noted American economist arranged a banquet to celebrate the man's many years of private and public contributions to the nation's thinking. When the festivities ended a group of newspaper reporters asked the guest of honor if he did not have a message for the people—perhaps some great economic truth distilled from his years of study.

"Well," said the economist, "there are a number of economic truths pertinent to these days, but they are rather complex and difficult to express in terms most people would understand. However, they all boil down to one simple fact that history has time and again proved:

There is no such thing as a free lunch."

Never Satisfied

A tourist in Mexico stopped to watch the village women do their laundry in hot springs and cold springs that were side by side, washing their clothes in one spring and rinsing them in the other. "Nature is pretty generous," said the tourist to his Mexican friend.

"Yes," replied the Mexican, "but most of these people complain because Nature doesn't give free soap."

Wealth

A man crossing the desert became separated from the caravan with which he had been traveling. All day long he wandered aimlessly under the searing sun, his exhaustion increasing and his thirst bringing him to a state of hopelessness. Suddenly he spotted what appeared to be a waterskin. He fell upon it, tore it open and found it worthless. It contained only twenty beautiful, flawless pearls.

Storm-tested

A tourist stood on the river bank watching a lumberman hook and pull out of the stream certain of the logs that came floating down the swift-flowing waters. Finally the observer asked the worker why certain of the logs were drawn off from the rest, especially since they all looked alike.

"They may look alike," said the lumberman, "but they are not. Most of the logs have grown on the mountainside and have been protected. They're only good for lumber. But these I've pulled aside are from the top of the mountain. They have been taking the brunt of the storms for years, and survived. They have grown up strong and have a finer grain. They will be used for special work."

Reality

Abraham Lincoln was walking one day along a street in Springfield with his two young sons, both of whom were crying. "Why, Mr. Lincoln," exclaimed a passer-by, "what is the matter with the children?"

"The same thing that's wrong with the rest of the world," replied Lincoln. "I've got three walnuts and each boy wants two."

Buried Treasure

A farmer on his deathbed summoned his four sons and told them that he was leaving his farm to them in four equal parts. "I have very little ready cash, but you will find that the greater part of my wealth is buried somewhere in the ground, about a foot and a half from the surface. I have forgotten precisely where." Then he died.

The four sons set to work on the fields and dug up every inch of them, searching for the treasure the father had buried. They found nothing. But they decided that so long as they dug up all the ground, they might as well sow a crop and reap a good harvest.

That autumn, after an abundant harvest, the four boys again began digging in search of the buried treasure; as a consequence their farm was turned over more thoroughly than any other farm in the area.

And of course again they reaped a fine harvest. After they had repeated this procedure for several more years, the four sons finally realized what their father had meant when he told them that his wealth was buried in the ground.

AESOP

Habit

Every night for years the lighthouse keeper went to sleep to the restless, unceasing, lonely sound of the bell on the buoy near the lighthouse. In fact, he was never conscious of the ceaseless tolling of the bell as it rolled and rocked with the motions of the sea.

One night, however, the bell suddenly ceased ringing. Immediately the lighthouse keeper sat up in bed and, startled, said to his wife: "What was that?"

The Sword of Damocles

Several hundred years before the Christian era the Greek city of Syracuse in Sicily was tyrannized by King Dionysius, a man of considerable ability but of strange and capricious tempers. One day his friend Damocles said he thought nothing better could be imagined than the dignity and pleasure of being a king. Dionysius decided to take him at his word and teach him a lesson. He ordered that a great banquet be prepared, at which Damocles would be the guest of honor, arrayed in the royal raiment and seated upon the king's own throne.

Damocles was delighted with the honor paid him and the attention lavished upon him—the magnificent food, rare wines, abundant flowers, perfumes, music, and the slavish service. In the midst of these festivities he happened to glance upwards. There, almost touching his head, was a massive and glistening sword hanging by a single horsehair. The slightest jar would cause the sword to drop on the head of the honored guest.

Thus did Dionysius teach Damocles the constant dread in which the tyrant lived.

The Arab and His Camel

One night when the desert winds blew hard and cold a camel pushed his nose through the flap of an Arab's tent and said: "Because it's so cold out here would you mind if I just kept my nose in your tent?" The Arab agreed and went back to sleep.

Later in the evening he awoke and discovered the camel had not only his nose, but also his head and shoulders in the tent. When the camel pleaded, the kindly Arab allowed the beast to put his forelegs into the tent, too. Then the camel said, "It's getting colder. Why not let me come entirely into your tent?"

"Certainly," said the easy-going Arab, "come on in."

Before dawn the Arab awoke stiff with cold and covered with sand blown by the desert wind. He was outside the tent. The camel was sleeping comfortably inside the tent.

The Inner Light

Two children living happily in their father's house would often look at evening to another house standing on a distant hilltop. The evening sun painted it with glory as its rays were reflected from many window-panes. One afternoon they started out to visit the house of the golden windows. They struggled over fields and through brush and woodland until at last the moment arrived. They stood before the enchanted house of their dreams and their hopes. But alas! they found it deserted and bleak. Dust and slime of many years had covered the panes of glass. They gave forth no golden splendor. The house was lonely, cold, forsaken. Disappointed, discouraged, afraid, they turned to go. As they did so their eyes fell on their own home in the distance bathed in the golden splendor of the setting sun.

They saw this and more than this. Their sad experience had taught them to realize the inner light, not the reflected light, which shines in every home worthy of the name and makes it one of the brightest and dearest spots on earth, a refuge, a joy, a hope, and forever a happiness. But it was under the spell of the light reflected from its windows that they caught the full vision of the inner and true light and glory of home. And they both cried out: "See our house; our own home is the true house of the golden windows!"

IGNATIUS W. COX

The Cheater

A baker in a small town regularly bought a fairly large amount of butter from a neighboring farmer. One day the baker suspected the butter was not the weight he ordered and paid for. His scales confirmed his suspicion. Thereafter the baker weighed all the butter from the farmer and found he was getting less and less than he paid for. Finally he had the farmer arrested on a charge of fraud.

At the trial it was revealed that the farmer had no scales. The astonished judge asked the farmer how he could weigh the butter without scales.

"It's this way, judge," said the farmer. "When the baker began to buy butter from me I began to buy bread from him. I buy his one pound loaf and I always use that as the weight for my butter. So, if the weight of my butter is wrong it is only because the weight of his bread is wrong. If I have been cheating him it is only because he has been cheating me."

"Case dismissed!" said the judge.

Education

One night three horsemen were riding across the desert. When they came to the dry bed of a river a voice came out of the darkness, and said, "Halt!"

The men obeyed the command of the hidden voice. The voice then said, "You have done as I commanded. Now get off your horses, pick up a handful of pebbles, put the pebbles into your pockets, remount your horses, and continue on your journey." Then the voice added, "Since you have done as I commanded, tomorrow at sunup you will be both glad and sorry that you obeyed me."

Mystified, the three horsemen rode on through the night. When the sun arose the horsemen reached into their pockets and found that a miracle had happened. The pebbles in their pockets had been transformed into magnificent diamonds, rubies and other precious stones. They remembered the warning, that they would be both glad and sorry; glad that they had taken some pebbles, sorry that they had not taken more.

Gifts

An angel was visiting a city, observing people without being observed. One night he noted a hungry newsboy fallen asleep. A young lady came along with a male companion. Seeing the newsboy, she shyly in her pity dropped a sixpence into his pocket and was coming away when the young man with her gave another sixpence and an old lady standing by gave threepence and another young man, though not very heartily, handed in a shilling. So that, after all had been quietly slipped into the little sleeper's pocket, he had received two shillings and threepence. Delighted, the angel flew away to notify the great recording angel about the good deed he had just witnessed. "I know, I know"; said the recording angel, "see, it is all written down already, as the Lord told me," and he showed him the book. But there was only ninepence recorded, "Because," as he went on to explain, "that young maiden gave sixpence out of her love, and the aged lady gave threepence out of pity, but the young escort gave because he wanted to be thought well of by the young lady, and the other young man gave because he did not want to be thought mean. These last two do not count."   RALPH W. SOCKMAN

The Tail of the Dog

An old South African native was told he had to be taxed because the government, like a father, protected him from enemies, cared for him when he was sick, fed him when he was hungry, gave him an education and, for these reasons, needed money.

Taking it all in, the old native replied slowly:

"Yes, I understand. It is like this: I have a dog and the dog is hungry. He comes to me and begs food. I say to him, 'My dear faithful dog, I see you are very hungry. I am sorry for you. I shall give you meat.'

"I then take a knife, cut off the dog's tail, give it to him, and say: 'Here, my faithful dog, be nourished by this nice piece of meat.'"

Secondhand Information

Secondhand information is not always reliable; one cannot blindly assume another person is correct. For instance, the telephone operator in a small town received a call every day in which she was asked the time of day. Finally the operator asked her mysterious caller who he was and why he called every day to learn what time it was.

"Oh," said the caller, "I'm the fellow who blows the noon whistle at the town hall, and I just want to be sure I'm right on the second."

"And we here in the exchange," said the operator between hearty laughs, "set our watches and clocks by the town whistle!"

A Wasted Day

Mencius, the great disciple of Confucius, was raised with great care by his mother. She was determined that he should become an honorable man who respected life and performed well his duties in it.

One day while the very watchful mother sat weaving, young Mencius arrived home from school and greeted his mother with all the respect he had been taught to pay her.

"How did you progress in school today, my son?" she asked.

"Oh, well enough I suppose," the youth answered with lazy indifference.

The mother said nothing. Instead she picked up a knife and with swift motion she cut through the warp and woof of the cloth she had woven.

Startled by so extraordinary an act, Mencius asked his mother why she had done so.

"I have only done to the piece of cloth I was weaving

today, what you have done to your life today," replied the mother.

Perspective

A politician was enraged when he read what he regarded as a slanderous attack on his character and competence.

But one of his advisers urged him to calm down and consider the question analytically. "Bear in mind," he said, "there are 20,000 people in this town. One-half of them don't get this paper. That leaves 10,000. One-half of those who get the paper didn't see the story. That leaves 5,000. One-half of those who saw it, don't believe it. That leaves 2,500. One-half of those who believe it, don't know you. That leaves 1,250. One-half of those who know you are your friends. That leaves 625. One-half of those felt that way about you before they read the story. So there's really nothing to get excited about."

The Sparrow

I was returning from hunting, walking along the avenue of the garden, my dog running in front of me.

Suddenly she took shorter steps, and began to steal along as though tracking game.

I looked along the avenue, and saw a young sparrow, with yellow about its beak and down on its head. It had fallen out of the nest (the wind was violently shaking the birch-trees in the avenue) and sat unable to move, helplessly flapping its half-grown wings.

My dog was slowly approaching it, when, suddenly darting down from a tree close by, an old dark-throated sparrow fell like a stone right before his nose, and all ruffled up, terrified, with despairing and pitiful cheeps, it flung itself twice towards the open jaws of shining teeth.

It sprang to save; it cast itself before its nestling.... all its tiny body was shaking with terror; its note was harsh and strange. Swooning with fear, it offered itself up!

What a huge monster must the dog have seemed to it! and yet it could not stay on its high branch out of danger.... A force stronger than its will flung it down.

My dog Tresor stood still, drew back.... Clearly he too recognized this force.

I hastened to call off the disconcerted dog, and went away full of reverence.

Yes; do not laugh; I felt reverence for that tiny heroic bird, for its impulse of love.

Love, I thought, is stronger than death or the fear of death. Only by it, by love, life holds together and advances.

IVAN TURGENEV

The Rainbow

The late William T. Ellis once described the Niagara River as "a parable of the beautifying of disaster." The Niagara River is not one of the great rivers of the world. Running from Lake Erie to Lake Ontario, it is only a few miles long. But what makes the river significant is that at Niagara Falls there is a tragedy in the channel—a break in the even flow of the stream, so that the waters make a stupendous leap into the gorge below. As they are shattered and bruised on the rocks beneath the falls, however, there is cast up into the sunlight the exquisite rainbow of the Niagara, which even kings and queens come from the ends of the earth to see.

Life is like that. Suddenly we have to make a blind leap of faith into an overwhelming abyss of suffering. Completely shattered on the cruel rocks of reality, our emotions are churned into a seething foam of bewilderment. But out of our distresses there is cast up the sunlight of God's love, a rainbow of penitence, hope and trust—a radiance in the midst of our tears.

EDWIN T. DAHLBERG

When the Wind Blows

A sturdy but diffident young man asked a farmer for a job as a farm hand.

"What can you do?" inquired the farmer.

"I can do whatever has to be done, and I can sleep when the wind blows," replied the applicant.

Although mystified by the phrase "sleep when the wind blows," the farmer did not press the question but hired the young man.

Some nights later a violent storm awoke the farmer. He got up and tried unsuccessfully to arouse the farm hand, then with considerable annoyance went out himself to see if all was well. He found the barn locked, the chicken coop properly closed up, a wagonload of hay covered with a tarpaulin which was securely battened down, and all else in a condition of safety from the elements. Then the farmer realized what his new farm hand meant when he said: "I can sleep when the wind blows."

Rich Man Redistributes His Wealth

In the course of an interview with a journalist of advanced economic views who had been critical of him, Andrew Carnegie rebuked his interviewer for his "equal distribution of wealth" theories.

The journalist replied with vigor, reminding Carnegie of his own hoarded millions in the midst of great poverty and suffering.

The Scotch steel magnate listened for a few minutes and then asked his secretary to bring from the file a statement of the Carnegie total wealth. The millionaire showed the statement to the journalist, did some quick figuring on a scratch pad, reached into his pocket and handed the interviewer thirteen cents: "Here, sir, is your share of my wealth."

Where the Taxes Went

When a king discovered that the finances of his kingdom were dangerously depleted he called in his 25 chief deputies to examine and solve the crisis.

"Why," asked the king, "is our treasury empty when we collect so much in taxes? What happens to the money? Can it be large-scale thieving?"

Everyone looked to the Secretary of the Treasury for a reply. This sage gentleman excused himself briefly and returned with a large piece of ice, saying "This will answer your question."

The Secretary handed the ice to one man, told him to hold it briefly in his hands and then pass it along to the person next to him. The ice went from man to man, steadily melting. When it reached the king the ice was so diminished he could close his hand over it.

"That, sire," said the Secretary of the Treasury, "is what happens to the taxes we collect."

Man Meets Man **3**

I sought my soul —
but my soul I could not see;
I sought my God —
but my God eluded me;
I sought my brother —
and found all three.

AUTHOR UNKNOWN

A Brother in Distress

In this skeptical world miracles can still occur, when men act their faith as well as preach it, and love gets a chance to show its power. As in the curious adventure of the famous East Indian missionary, Sadhu Subhar Singh.

One afternoon the Far Eastern Christian was climbing a mountain road in Tibet. With him traveled a bonze, a Buddhist monk. The two wayfarers were well aware that a storm was rising and that they must reach a certain monastery before dark or perish in piercing mountain cold. As they hastened forward in the icy wind they passed a precipice from which rose a groaning voice; at the bottom lay a fallen man, badly hurt and unable to move. The Tibetan said:

"In my belief, here we see Karma; this is the work of Fate, the effect of a cause. This man's doom is to die here, while I must press on upon my own errand."

But the Christian answered: "In my belief, I must go to my brother's aid."

So the Tibetan hurried on his way, while Sadhu clambered down the slope, packed the man on his back, and struggled upward again to the darkening road. His body was dripping with perspiration when at last he came in sight of the lights of the monastery. Then he stumbled and nearly fell over an object on the ground, and stood, overwhelmed with pity and amazement. Huddled at his feet lay his Tibetan companion, frozen to death. But Sadhu had escaped the same doom because his hard exercise in carrying an injured brother on his back kept his body warm, and saved his life. FULTON OURSLER

The Magic Sticks

When an Oriental prince awoke one morning and discovered some of his costly possessions were missing, he summoned his wise men and asked them to find the thief. Most of the wise men did no more than suggest the obvious procedures.

But the wisest of the wise men said: "I'll find the thief with my magic sticks. When one of these sticks is placed near a thief overnight the stick grows two inches. Put your servants in separate cells tonight and I will put a magic stick in each cell. In the morning the thief will be revealed." The prince agreed to this.

The next morning the sticks were gathered and measured, and one stick was found to be two inches *shorter* than the others. "What kind of nonsense is this?" demanded the prince. "You said one of the sticks would grow longer?"

"True, your majesty, that is what I *said*. Nevertheless, it has worked as I expected. There is the thief," and he pointed to the man who had handed in the shorter stick.

The accused servant promptly confessed, explaining that he knew if any of the sticks grew longer it would be the one in his cell. "The agony I went through last night was terrible," he said. "I kept looking at this stick to see if it would expose me, and I thought I saw it begin to grow. I became so utterly convinced, in my guilt, that it was increasing in length, that finally I cut off two inches so it would be the same size as the others."

This wise man knew the workings of conscience.

Practical Sympathy

Years ago in the English town of Rochdale Jacob Bright, a mill owner and father of the famous statesman John Bright, was walking up the hill from town to his home, when he encountered a poor farmer in serious trouble. The poor man's horse had broken a leg and had to be destroyed. People stood around the distraught farmer telling him how sorry they were at his great loss. As soon as Jacob Bright took in the situation he removed his hat, placed five pounds in it and said to the sympathetic bystanders: "I'm sorry five pounds for our neighbor. How sorry are you?" He then passed the hat and collected enough money for the man to buy another horse.

A True Gentleman

An explorer describes an expedition that recently visited the Negritos of the Philippines—an undernourished race, harmless as children and gentle of disposition: "The trip entailed a long hike up a mountain, with the thermometer at 125 degrees. I could not eat and could hardly breathe. My companions spread a lunch under the trees. As they ate, an old man, hideous and blotched with sores, approached and looked on. 'There is the most hideous human being I have ever seen. I have traveled in South America, Africa and all over the South Seas, and I have never seen a human being nearer an animal than that old beast', said a newspaper man. Suddenly, the old fellow disappeared and returned with a huge palm leaf for a fan; and, noting me ill, pointed to me to lie down. He disappeared again, and returned with a tube of spring water and filled a bamboo cup for me to drink from. After lunch was over, one of the party gave him a sandwich. He looked at it hungrily, but gave it to a mother with a child. Another given him, he handed to a timid old woman. The third he gave a hungry old man. More he passed around, until all of the starving group had been fed. Finally he ate. And yet, only a few moments before we Caucasians, in our wisdom, had decided that this ugly old man was the nearest to animal of any human being that we had seen."

True Unity

At the height of his conquests the Chan of Cathay fell ill and feared that he was going to die. He called his twelve sons to him and ordered each of them to bring to him one of his arrows. Then he commanded that the twelve arrows should be bound tightly together in three places. When this had been done he told his oldest son to break the bundle of arrows, which the lad tried to do with all his strength, but failed. The Chan gave the same instruction to the second son, and each son after that, but not one of them could break the bundle of arrows.

Then the Chan told the youngest son to remove the binding from the arrows, and to break each arrow separately, which the boy did easily.

"But why," asked the Chan of the oldest son, "could not you or your brothers break the arrows, as your youngest brother did?"

"Because when we tried to break them they were united, but he broke them because they were separated," replied the older sons.

"My sons," said the Chan, "truly thus will it fare by you. For as long as ye be bound together in three places, that is to say, in love, in truth and in good accord, no man shall be of power to grieve you. But if ye be dissevered from these three places, that one not help the other, ye shall be destroyed and brought to nought. And if each of you love one another and help each other, ye shall be lords and sovereigns of all others." And having said this the Chan died.

Snap Judgment

During World War Two an Army captain lined up his men in company formation and explained that twenty volunteers were needed immediately for a desperate undertaking. He pulled no punches, explaining in detail the nature and extreme hazards involved. He asked any men willing to undergo this perilous mission to step forward three paces.

At the instant he finished this statement he was handed an urgent message from headquarters, which he read and acknowledged with a penciled notation.

When the captain turned again to his company he found the lines unbroken by even a single man, and he began wrathfully to excoriate them for indifference, lack of spirit and poor patriotism.

"But, sir," interjected a first lieutenant, "the entire company moved forward three paces while you were reading the despatch. Every man wants to volunteer."

Community

A preacher in a rural community heard that a man in his parish had announced that he would no longer attend church services because he had decided he could commune with God just as easily in his fields and garden and among his trees.

One autumn evening the preacher called on his reluctant parishioner, and for a while the two men sat before the blazing fireplace saying little or nothing, and not a word about church attendance. The man waited uneasily for the preacher to broach the subject. The preacher was aware that he would be expected to rebuke the man.

Finally the preacher picked up the tongs, lifted a single glowing coal from the fire and set it down on the hearth, and silently waited until the coal quickly ceased burning while the other coals in the fire continued to burn brightly. "You see what happens," said the preacher.

"You need say no more," replied the man. "Man cannot live alone. I'll be at church next Sunday."

Tolerance

Legend has it that when Abraham sat at his tent door, according to his custom, waiting to entertain strangers, he espied an old man, stooping and leaning on his staff. He was weary with age and travail, being a hundred years of age. Abraham received him kindly, washed his feet, provided supper, and caused him to sit down. Observing that the old man ate and prayed not, nor begged a blessing on his meat, Abraham asked him why he did not worship the God of heaven. The old man told him that he worshipped the fire only, and acknowledged no other God. At this answer Abraham grew so zealously angry, that he threw the old man out of his tent, and exposed him to all the evils of the night in an unguarded condition. When the old man was gone, God called Abraham, and asked him where the stranger was. "I thrust him away, because he did not worship thee." God answered him, "I have suffered him these hundred years, though he dishonored me; and wouldst thou not endure him one night, when he gave thee no trouble?"

JEREMY TAYLOR

True Charity

China was in the lethal grip of famine—a more severe one than customarily visits that nation.

Won Chang and his wife, poor even in good times, were in desperate straits, with hardly more than a handful of rice left. At that moment a neighbor came and appealed to them for help. He was starving.

Won's wife argued, "If we give this neighbor from our handful of food we will surely die."

"But," said Won, "If we don't give him some food it will only postpone our deaths one day; perhaps we shall die tomorrow. But, our neighbor will die today."

The Three Experts

One day a lawyer, a certified public accountant and a management engineer were lunching together and decided to pool their brains, talents, experience and savings in a business venture of their own.

But their venture failed to reap the riches envisioned. Puzzled and discouraged they agreed to sell the business and dissolve their partnership. A buyer appeared, the sale was concluded and the former partners went their separate ways to other endeavors.

Months later the three men sat again at lunch and fell to wondering why their venture had failed. They determined to call on the man who bought the business and inquire of him its condition.

They found their successor to be busy, apparently prosperous and obviously happy.

"How did you do it?" chorused the astonished trio.

"Really fellows, I'm not sure I can explain. I couldn't operate the business with all your theories about ratios, depreciation, surveys, saturation points, laws of diminishing returns, per man-hour productivity, and all the rest. I don't understand these things. I just had to run this outfit on the basis that it costs me two dollars to produce the article and I have to sell it for at least three dollars to make a fair profit. I'm doing that so I'm makin' a good living out of it."

"Six Pennyworth of Miracle"

George Gissing was going along the road one day, and he saw a poor little lad, perhaps ten years old, crying bitterly. He had lost sixpence with which he had been sent to pay a debt. "Sixpence dropped by the wayside, and a whole family made wretched. I put my hand into my pocket, and wrought six pennyworth of miracle."

I think Gissing's phrase is very significant. It suggests how easily some miracles can be wrought. How many troubled, crooked, miserable conditions there are which are just waiting the arrival of some simple, human ministry and they will be immediately transformed! . . .

John Morel, Mayor of Darlington, was passing through the town and met a fellow citizen who had just been released from jail, where he had served three years for embezzlement. "Hallo!" said the Mayor, in his own cheery tone. "I'm glad to see you! How are you!" Little else was said, for the man seemed ill at ease. Years afterwards, as John Morel told me, the man met him in another town, and immediately said, "I want to thank you for what you did for me when I came out of prison." "What did I do?" "You spoke a kind word to me and it changed my life!" Six penny-worth of miracle!

JOHN HENRY JOWETT

The Banker and The Beggar

A series of reverses had deprived him of money, possessions and finally of self-respect. He turned despairingly to begging—extending an unsure hand with a few pencils in it at subway stations in downtown Manhattan.

One day an elderly banker dropped a quarter in the beggar's trembling hand, turned to go, hesitated and then wheeled on the mendicant with: "I want to apologize for treating you as a beggar. You are a merchant, of course, and I came back to get the pencil I paid for." The astonished peddler handed the banker five pencils and thanked him with wondering warmth.

Many months later the banker stopped into a small stationery store on the outer fringe of the Wall Street area. As he was about to leave after making a few minor purchases the proprietor stopped him and said: "I'm sure you won't remember me, but I will never forget you. Some time ago I was a subway beggar with a handful of pencils and you treated me as a business man—a 'merchant' you called me. That remark gave me back my self-respect. From then on I refused gifts and really sold pencils—lots of them and good ones, too. From this sidewalk business I saved my money, borrowed a bit more, and then opened this little shop. I'm beginning to make a go of it. And all because of a few words from you."

He Spoke Too Soon

A friend took a boastful skeptic to Madame Tussaud's famous Wax Works, in London, where characters and episodes from history are reproduced with astonishing fidelity to life. As they passed into the exhibit the skeptic pointed to the figure of a policeman and grudgingly admitted "Now this representation of a policeman is pretty lifelike, but of course an expert can spot several deficiencies."

The critic collapsed when the figure reacted to the remark by raising an eyebrow in annoyance.

Lincolnian Perspective

Several days before he was assassinated, Abraham Lincoln received a request from General Creswell for a pardon for a Confederate friend, and replied:

Creswell, you make me think of a lot of young folks who once started out Maying. To reach their destination, they had to cross a shallow stream, and did so by means of an old flat-boat. When the time came to return, they found to their dismay that the old scow had disappeared. They were in sore trouble, and thought over all manner of devices for getting over the water, but without avail.

After a time, one of the boys proposed that each fellow should pick up the girl he liked best and wade over with her. The masterly proposition was carried out, until all that were left upon the island was a little short chap and a great, gothic-built, elderly lady.

Now, Creswell, you are trying to leave me in the same predicament. You fellows are getting all your own friends out of this scrape; and you will succeed in carrying off one after another, until nobody but Jeff Davis and myself will be left on the island, and then I won't know what to do. How should I feel? How should I look, lugging him over?

Man Falters, Man Advances

4

Behold the turtle.
He makes progress
only when he sticks his neck out.

JAMES BRYANT CONANT

One Man

A man who had got himself into a precarious state of mind because of his conviction that one person—and himself in particular—was of little consequence in the world, took a trip by sea in the hope of ridding himself of his melancholy.

One dark evening at sea, shortly after he had gone to bed, he heard the cry "Man overboard!" He was in his pajamas, he could not swim or man a lifeboat; what could he do? He reached for his flashlight and directed its beam from the porthole upon the sea. The light fell upon the man in the water, to whom a life preserver was then thrown, and a life was saved.

A Speckled Ax

My scheme of ORDER gave me the most trouble. Order with regard for places for things, papers, etc., I found extremely difficult to acquire. . . . I made so little progress in amendment, and had such frequent relapses, that I was almost ready to give up the attempt, and content myself with a faulty character in that respect, like the man who, in buying an ax of a smith, my neighbor, desired to have the whole of its surface as bright as the edge. The smith consented to grind it bright for him if he would turn the wheel; he turn'd, while the smith press'd the broad face of the ax hard and heavily on the stone, which made the turning of it very fatiguing. The man came every now and then from the wheel to see how the work went on, and at length would take his ax as it was, without farther grinding. "No," said the smith, "turn on, turn on; we shall have it bright by-and-by; as yet it is only speckled." "Yes," says the man, *"but I think I like a speckled ax best."* And I believe this may have been the case with many, who, having for want of some such means as I employ'd, found the difficulty of obtaining good and breaking bad habits in other points of vice and virtue, have given up the struggle, and concluded that *"a speckled ax was best."*

BENJAMIN FRANKLIN

The Untouched Heart

Among the students at a college was a young man on crutches. Although not a handsome fellow, he had a talent for friendliness and optimism, and he earned many scholastic honors and had the respect of his classmates. One day a new student asked him what had caused him to become so badly crippled.

"Infantile paralysis," replied the genial young man.

"With a misfortune like that," exclaimed the other fellow, "how can you face the world so confidently and so happily?"

"Oh," replied the polio victim, "the disease never touched my heart."

Bits and Pieces

The man in charge of building a great cathedral was pestered repeatedly by an apprentice who wanted to design and arrange the glass for just one of the windows. Although he did not want to discourage so laudable an ambition, neither did the boss want to risk the waste of costly material. Finally he told the apprentice that he could try his hand on one small window, but that he would have to provide the material for it himself.

Undaunted, the apprentice gathered up all the bits and pieces of glass that had been cut off and discarded by other workmen, and with these scraps he worked out a design of rare beauty. When the cathedral was opened to the public, people stood in awe before the one small window designed by the apprentice.

Capacity and Goal

Jim Corbett, the former world's heavyweight champion, used to tell of the day he was out doing road work for an upcoming fight, when he came upon a man fishing and stopped to watch him. The fisherman tugged at his line and pulled in a large trout, examined it and threw it back in the water. Then he pulled in a large perch, unhooked it and also threw it back. On the third try the fisherman pulled in a small trout, which he put into his creel and prepared to depart.

Corbett asked him why he had thrown the larger fish back into the water and kept the small one. "Small frying pan" replied the fisherman.

Trust Your Own Judgment

An artisan, aware of his ability but unhappy because of his obscurity, determined to bid for fame and wealth by casting the finest bell possible. But try as he did to achieve renown and money, something always proved wrong with the succession of bells through which he hoped to win the prize.

Finally the bell maker decided that fame and wealth were not for him, and that furthermore these were not all they were said to be. "However," he said, "I'm going to make one more bell—a bell that I will enjoy making and enjoy hearing and having. I'm going to satisfy myself for a change."

When the bell was finished those who heard it hailed its perfection of tone, its thrilling beauty. As a result the bell maker became famous and rich.

Inordinate Ambition

To what end do men gather riches, but to multiply more? Do they not like Pyrrhus, the King of Epire, add house to house and land to lands, that they may get it all? A story is told of that prince that having conceived a purpose to invade Italy he sent for Cineas, a philosopher and the king's friend. Cineas asked him to what purpose would he invade Italy? He said, "to conquer it." "And what will you do when you have conquered it?" "Go into France," said the king, "and conquer that." "And what will you do when you have conquered France?" "Conquer Germany." "And what then?" said the philosopher. "Conquer Spain." "I perceive," said Cineas, "you mean to conquer all the world. What will you do when you have conquered all?" "Why then," said the king, "we will return and enjoy ourselves in quiet in our own land." "So you may now," said the philosopher, "without all this ado."

THOMAS TRAHERNE

Trifles

A friend once called on Michelangelo just as he was putting the finishing touches on one of his great works of sculpture. Some time later the friend again visited the great artist and, to his astonishment, found Michelangelo still at work on the same statue but with no obvious difference so far as he could determine.

"Have you been away since I saw you last?" he asked the artist.

"By no means," said Michelangelo. "I have been retouching this part, and polishing that, softening this feature and strengthening that muscle—and so on."

"But," said the visitor, "these are only trifles."

"That may be," said the artist. "But bear in mind that trifles make perfection, and perfection is no trifle."

The Answer

The Reverend Margaret Blair Johnstone, Congregational minister of Groton, Connecticut, tells of a young widow who had determined upon self-destruction because, she said, "I cannot go on without him. What have I to live for? This is the greatest blow in the world."

"Then," said Mrs. Johnstone, "why do you want to inflict it on your mother and your children?"

"But what have I to live for?" the woman moaned.

"You might turn to God and ask. He has a purpose. He is not aimless, I assure you. If you seek Him, he'll show you why He wants you to live."

Fourteen years later that same widow hurried to her nineteen-year-old daughter's bedside.

"I don't want to live," the girl moaned in her first shock of knowledge that her husband had been killed in a highway accident which terminated their honeymoon. "I can't take it," she repeated. "What have I to live for without him, tell me, Mother?"

It was then, and only then, that the older widow knew she had found her own answer.

GRACE PERKINS OURSLER
and APRIL ARMSTRONG

The Queen Introduces Alice to A Condition of Modern Life

Alice never could quite make out, in thinking it over afterwards, how it was that they began; all she remembers is that they were running hand in hand, and the Queen went so fast that it was all she could do to keep up with her; and still the Queen kept crying "Faster! Faster!" but Alice felt she *could not* go faster, though she had no breath left to say so.

The most curious part of the thing was, that the trees and other things round them never changed their places at all; however fast they went, they never seemed to pass anything. "I wonder if all the things move along with us?" thought poor, puzzled Alice. And the Queen seemed to guess her thoughts, for she cried, "Faster! Don't try to talk!"

Not that Alice had any idea of doing *that*. She felt as if she would never be able to talk again, she was getting so much out of breath; and still the Queen cried, "Faster! Faster!" and dragged her along.

"Nearly there?" the Queen repeated. "Why we passed it ten minutes ago. Faster!" And they ran on for a time in silence, with the wind whistling in Alice's ears, and almost blowing her hair off her head, she fancied.

"Now! Now!" cried the Queen. "Faster! Faster!" And they went so fast that at last they seemed to skim through the air, hardly touching the ground with their feet, till suddenly, just as Alice was getting quite exhausted, they stopped, and she found herself sitting on the ground, breathless and giddy.

The Queen propped her up against a tree, and said kindly, "You may rest a little now."

Alice looked around her in great surprise. "Why, I believe we've been under this tree the whole time! Everything's just as it was!"

"Of course it is," said the Queen; "What would you have it?"

"Well, in *our* country," said Alice, still panting a little, "you'd generally get to somewhere else—if you

Man
Falters
Man
Advances

65

ran very fast for a long time, as we've been doing."

"A slow sort of country!" said the Queen. "Now *here*, you see, it takes all the running *you* can do, to keep in the same place. If you want to get somewhere else you must run at least twice as fast as that!"

LEWIS CARROLL

Opportunity

An unusually successful business man was invited to address a group of younger executives on the subject of opportunities. He began his talk by tacking to the wall a big sheet of white paper and placing a black dot in the middle of the sheet.

"What do you see?" he asked pointing to the paper on the wall.

"A black spot" called out every man in the audience.

"Yes, I see a black dot, too," replied the speaker. "But none of you saw the much greater expanse of white. This is the point of my talk on opportunities."

Perfection

Idlers of the seacoast town watched the village smith day after day as he painstakingly wrought every link of a great chain he was forging. Behind his back they scoffed at such care being taken on so ordinary a thing as a chain. But the fine old craftsman worked on, ignoring them as if he had not heard them at all.

Eventually that conscientiously made chain was fastened to a great anchor on the deck of an ocean vessel. For months it was never put to use. But one day the vessel was disabled by a breakdown of its steering apparatus while near the coast during a storm. Only a secure anchorage could prevent the vessel being driven onto the rocky coast. Thus the fate of the ship and its hundreds of passengers depended on the strength of that chain—the chain attached to the anchor.

Few aboard the ship saw much chance of the chain withstanding the weight of the ship when the violent sea pounded against her. But, then, they did not know of the care and skill lavished on each link of that chain by an obscure smith intent only on doing his best. And his best was good enough. The chain held; the ship and its passengers and crew survived.

The Eternal Tidal Force

I am told that when the great Hellgate Bridge was being built over the East River in New York the engineers came upon an old derelict ship, lying imbedded in the river mud, just where one of the central piers of the bridge was to go down to its bedrock foundation. No tugboat could be found that was able to start the derelict from its ancient bed in the ooze. It would not move, no matter what force was applied. Finally, with a sudden inspiration one of the workers hit upon this scheme. He took a large flat-boat, which had been used to bring stone down the river, and he chained it to the old sunken ship when the tide was low. Then he waited for the great tidal energies to do their work.

Slowly the rising tide, with all the forces of the ocean behind it and the moon above it, came up under the flat-boat, raising it inch by inch. And as it came up, lifted by irresistible power, the derelict came up with it, until it was entirely out of the mud that had held it. Then the boat, with its subterranean load, was towed out to sea where the old water-logged ship was unchained and allowed to drop forever out of sight and reach.

There are greater forces than those tidal waves waiting for us to use for our tasks. They have always been there. They are there now. But they do not *work*, they do not *operate,* until we lay hold of them and use them for our present purposes. We must be co-workers with God.

RUFUS M. JONES

Man Seeks God 5

The place where man vitally finds God . . .
is within his own experience
of goodness, truth and beauty.

HARRY EMERSON FOSDICK

A Man's Work

The zealous missionary had been preaching to the inhabitants of a certain town but seemed not to break through their wall of indifference. His apparent lack of success finally caused him great discouragement; he had gladly given up much to do this work, he had ignored the jibes of friends and the sneers of strangers; and now he was confronted with failure.

He went out into the countryside and sat down by the roadside exhausted, and fell asleep. He dreamed a vision of heaven, a land of contentment, peace and prosperity, and he heard a voice say to him, "My son, all this is yours." And he heard himself reply, "But Lord, I do not deserve it! My work has been a failure." "You deserve it," came the reply, "so long as you do the work of each day as well as you can." The missionary awoke and resumed his work, confident that out of apparent failure God would bring success.

Co-operation

A worried pastor of a small, struggling church dreamed one night a dream that on the following Sunday he related to his parishioners without embellishment or comment, nor did he need to. He related to them that in this dream he was driving his congregation in a bus up a steep hill, when suddenly the motor went dead. He got out and called to the passengers to come and help him. "I'll pull and you folks push and we'll all get to the top of the hill." So he went to the front of the bus and pulled and pulled. Perspiration poured from him and he gasped for breath, but the bus did not budge. He stopped to look behind him to see what the matter was. He found that the passengers in the bus had all remained in their seats.

God's Grace

An old woman was trudging along a country road with a heavy pack upon her back when her parson came along in his carriage and offered her a ride. Gratefully she climbed into the vehicle but kept the pack on her back. The clergyman suggested she put the pack on the floor of the carriage. The poor old lady said it was good enough of him to give her the lift but she did not think it fair to ask him to carry her burden too.

The minister quickly found in this a little sermon. He told the woman that this situation was somewhat like our relations with God. We believe that His grace can save our souls, but we fail to put our trust in His grace to help us with our daily burdens.

The Vital Link

A spider built his web in a barn, high up among the rafters, where he started by spinning a long, thin thread attached to the end of one of the beams. With this thread still attached to him, the spider jumped off the beam and spun out more thread on the way down, until he reached the place he planned as the center of his web. From the center he then spun out other threads like the spokes of a wheel, attaching each of them to the walls and other places. Finally he had an exquisitely made web, that helped him catch many fine fat flies. But he grew fat and lazy and vain.

One day he was admiring the web he had spun and he noticed the long fine thread he had first spun from the top beam and said, "I wonder what that is for? I can't imagine why I ever put it there—it doesn't catch any flies." And so on a sudden impulse he broke it. But as a result the whole wonderful web collapsed. The spider had forgotten that the one thread—the link to the strongest beam above—supported the whole web. It is very much the same when a man breaks his link with God.

Light from Above

A man being safely escorted through a dense forest one black night was puzzled and asked his guide how he could be so sure of the way when he couldn't see the path.

"I follow the path in the sky," replied the guide as he pointed to the thin line of light formed by an opening through the trees. "The light from on high," added the guide, "always keeps a man on the right road."

Faith

A blind man inched his way along the busy street during the rush hour, until he felt the curb with his foot. He paused until he sensed a person standing next to him, then he said: "May I accompany you across the street?" "Yes, certainly," came the reply from an elderly woman as she took his arm.

The two persons walked arm-in-arm safely across the street while cars and pedestrians swirled about them. When they came to the sidewalk on the other side of the street the blind man turned to thank his escort, but before he could phrase his appreciation she said, "Thanks for the safe crossing. Being blind is made bearable because of people's kindness."

"Faith! How wonderful faith is!" exclaimed the blind man.

Loyalty

One day a good-natured king gave a rare and beautiful fruit to a slave, who tasted it and thereupon said that never in his life had he eaten anything so delicious. This made the king wish to try it himself, and he asked the slave for a piece. But when he put it into his mouth he found it very bitter and he raised his eyebrows in astonishment. The slave said: "Sire, since I have received so many gifts at your hand how can I complain of one bitter fruit? Seeing that you shower benefits on me why should one bitterness estrange me from you?"   FARID UD-DIN ATTAR

The Heart's Door

When Holman Hunt's painting "The Light of the World" was unveiled an art critic thought he had found an error in this representation of Christ standing in a garden at midnight, holding a lantern in one hand and knocking on a door with the other hand.

"I say, Hunt," said the critic, "there is no handle on that door."

"That is correct," replied the artist. "You see, that is the door to the human heart; the door can only be opened from the inside."

God's Love

Charles Spurgeon, a noted English clergyman, noticed that the weather vane on the roof of a farm building bore the phrase "God is love" and was troubled. "Do you think God's love is as changeable as that weather vane?" he asked the farmer.

"You miss the point, sir," replied the farmer. "It's on the weather vane because no matter which way the wind is blowing, God is still love."

The Finger of God

The chaplain in a hospital was asked by a nurse to visit the man in room number 24, who was dying. The clergyman called on the young man and was surprised to find him sitting up in bed smoking and reading. The patient told the chaplain that he was in fine shape and was leaving the hospital the next day, and anyway needed no chaplain as he rejected religion.

The chaplain continued to chat with the man and gently persisted, as the result of which the young man then and there abandoned his pose of indifference and made his spiritual peace.

The next day the nurse said to the chaplain, "The man in room number 34 with whom you spent some time yesterday is much better this morning."

"I didn't visit the man in 34 yesterday," replied the chaplain. "You told me to visit 24, and I did!"

"How strange!" exclaimed the nurse. "The man in number 24 suddenly died during the night."

Communication

An Arab, a Persian, a Turk, and a Greek, agreed to get together for an evening meal, but when they met they quarreled as to what the meal should be. The Turk proposed Azum, the Arab Aneb, the Persian Anghur, while the Greek insisted on Staphylion.

While they were disputing
Before their eyes did pass
Laden with grapes, a gardener's ass.
Sprang to his feet each man, and showed,
With eager hand, that purple load.
"See Azum," said the Turk; and "See
Anghur," the Persian; "what could be
Better?" "Nay Aneb, Aneb 'tis,"
The Arab cried. The Greek said "This
Is my Staphylion." Then they bought
Their grapes in peace.
SIR EDWIN ARNOLD

Man's Dream
and Destiny   6

We are part of a creative destiny,
reaching backward and forward to infinity —
a destiny that reveals itself, though dimly,
in our striving, in our love,
our thought, our appreciation.

J. E. BOODIN

The Balancing of Memories

From ancient Greece comes the story of a woman who died and arrived at the River Styx to be ferried to the realm of departed spirits. Charon, the ferryman, told the woman that she was permitted to drink of the waters of Lethe if she wanted to forget the life she had just left. "Of course," added Charon, "you would then forget past joys as well as past sorrows."

"Then I would forget all I have suffered," said the woman.

"And your many occasions of rejoicing," reminded Charon.

"But my failures—I'd forget them, too," continued the woman.

"And also your triumphs," said Charon.

"And the times I have borne people's hatred," added the woman.

"True," said Charon, "but you also would forget how you have been loved."

The woman stopped to weigh the whole question, and finally decided not to sip of the waters of Lethe; it was not worth being rid of the memory of life's sorrows and failures, if one must at the same time lose the memory of life's happiness and love.

The Greater Fool

A potentate of ancient Asia presented his court jester with a beautifully wrought wand, and said: "Keep this until you find a greater fool than yourself."

The jester good-naturedly accepted the emblem of magic and flourished it on special occasions.

Some years later the ruler was dying and asked to see the jester, of whom he had grown fond.

"I wanted to say good-bye; I am going away on a long journey."

"Where are you going to?"

"I have no idea."

"How long will you be gone?"

"That I can tell you—it is forever. I know nothing more about this journey I am about to take."

"What have you done about providing for your well-being on this great trip?" asked the jester.

"Nothing whatever," replied the king. "There is nothing to be done."

"Since that is the way you feel," said the jester, "take this wand. You are the one to whom I should give it."

The Lamplighter

Harry Lauder, the famous singer, used to tell a story of his boyhood in Scotland. He liked to look from the window of his home during the gathering twilight, and watch the work of the lamplighter with his long pole with a torch on the end of it. The man went from street lamp to street lamp as he ascended the hilly street, leaving a trail of lights behind him. Then, as the road sloped downward, the lamplighter disappeared from view, but his torchlight could still be seen burning against the evening sky.

"That," as has been said by many people, "is what is meant by a genuine Christian: one who is a light to his fellowman while still living, and whose way has been marked by lights when he has left the world."

As Ye Sow

A wealthy man died and went to heaven. During his interview with St. Peter a beautiful mansion was pointed out to him. "That," said St. Peter, "is the celestial home of your butler."

"Well," smiled the new arrival broadly, "if my butler gets a place like that, I certainly look forward to seeing what my new home will be like."

"You will live in that little hut," said St. Peter.

"Me live in that hovel! It's ridiculous!" stormed the rich man.

"That is the best we can do for you," said St. Peter. "You must understand that we can only build your home up here with the materials you sent on ahead when you were on earth."

Two Ships

Two ships were once seen near land. One of them was leaving the harbor, and the other was coming into it. Everyone was cheering the outgoing ship, but the incoming ship was scarcely noticed.

A wise man standing nearby explained the people's reaction. "Rejoice not," he said, "over the ship that is setting out to sea, for you know not what destiny awaits it, what storms it may encounter, what dangers lurk before it. Rejoice rather over the ship that has reached port safely and brought back all its passengers in peace."

It is the way of the world, that when a human being is born, all rejoice; but when he dies, all sorrow. It should be the other way around. No one can tell what troubles await the developing child on its journey through life. But when a man has lived well and dies in peace, all should rejoice, for he has completed his journey successfully, and he is departing from this world with the imperishable crown.   MIDRASH

So Little Time

A man suddenly become rich bought a beautiful home in the country, furnished it lavishly, hired a tutor for his children, and invited many friends to a sumptuous housewarming.

During the housewarming the rich man observed that the tutor was having a gay time for himself, drinking glass after glass of the vintage champagne, dancing wildly with the ladies, telling his best stories, and singing all the songs he could recall.

Finally the master of the house could stand no more of this kind of behavior from one of his employees. He called the tutor aside and said to him: "What have you to be so happy about? Don't forget that your time in this house is limited."

"And you?" asked the tutor. "How long is your term for the enjoyment of all your wealth?"